All You Need to Know About Home Mortgage

How to Save Dollars on Your Home Mortgage

[RS Johnson]

Copyright © 2012 **RS Johnson**

All rights reserved.

Table of Contents

Introduction 5
Chapter 1| Main Types of Mortgages 7
   Fixed-Rate Mortgages 11
   Adjustable-Rate Mortgages 12
   First-Time Assistance Programs 12
   Mortgages for First-Time Buyers 13
Chapter 2| Loan Types 15
   Conventional Loans 15
   Federal Housing Administration (FHA) Loans 16
   V.A. Loans 17
   Requirements for Equity and Income 17
   Private Mortgage Insurance (PMI) 18
   Fixed-Rate Mortgages vs. Floating-Rate Mortgages
   20
Chapter 3| Mortgages for First-Time Buyers 22
   Understanding Conventional Mortgages and Loans
   22
   Conventional vs. Conforming 23
   How does a Conventional Mortgage or Loan Works?
   24
   Required Documentation 24

Interest Rates for Conventional Mortgages..........26

Special Factors to Consider When Obtaining a Conventional Mortgage or Loan..........................26

Chapter 4| Jumbo vs. Conventional Mortgages: An Overview 29

Jumbo Mortgages..29

Conventional Mortgages....................................31

Special Considerations 32

Chapter 5| What Is an Assumable Mortgage?.........34

Understanding Assumable Mortgages...................34

Types of Assumable Mortgages 35

Advantages and Disadvantages of Assumable Mortgages..36

Special Considerations for Assumable Mortgages .37

Conclusion 39

Introduction

Unlike commercial or industrial property, a home mortgage is a loan provided by the mortgage company, a bank, or other financial institution to purchase a home—either a primary residence, a secondary residence, or an investment residence. In a home mortgage, the property owner (the borrower) transfers title to the lender to understand that the title will be returned to the owner once the final loan payment is made and all other mortgage terms are met.

One of the most common and one of the most recommended types of debt is a home mortgage. Because mortgages are secured debt, they have lower interest rates than almost any other type of loan available to an individual consumer. There is an asset (the home) that serves as collateral for the loan.

Your mortgage payment is divided into two components: principal and interest. The loan amount is known as the principal. Lenders charge interest as a fee for the privilege of borrowing money that you can repay over time (calculated as a percentage of the principal). During the term of your mortgage, you make monthly payments based on an amortization schedule set by your lender.

Another factor in mortgage pricing is the annual percentage rate (APR), which calculates the total cost. The APR properly includes both the interest rate and any extra loan costs.

Home mortgages enable a far larger number of individuals to own real estate because the whole purchase price of the property does not have to be supplied up front. However, because the lender owns the home for the mortgage duration, it has the right to foreclose (take possession of it from the homeowner and sell it on the open market) if the borrower cannot make the payments.

A house mortgage's fixed or adjustable interest rate is paid monthly, along with the principal loan amount. The interest rate and monthly payment for a fixed-rate mortgage remain the same for each term. A home mortgage with an adjustable-rate fluctuates in terms of interest rate and monthly payment. Because the borrower risks an increase in interest rates, adjustable-rate home mortgage interest rates are generally lower than fixed-rate home mortgage interest rates.

In either case, the mortgage works the same way. However, as the homeowner pays down the principal over time, the interest is calculated smaller. This is because future mortgage payments go toward principal reduction rather than just interest charges.

Chapter 1 | Main Types of Mortgages

Not all mortgage products are created equal. Some regulations are more stringent than others. For example, some lenders may require a 20% down payment, while others may only require 3% of the home's purchase price. In addition, some types of loans require you to have perfect credit. Others are geared towards borrowers with less-than-perfect credit.

Although the federal government is not a lender, it does guarantee certain types of loans that meet strict income, loan limits, and geographic eligibility requirements. A list of possible mortgage loans is provided below.

Fannie And Freddie are two government-sponsored businesses in the United States that acquire and sell most conventional mortgages.

1. Conventional Mortgages

A conventional loan is not government-guaranteed. However, borrowers with strong credit, steady work and income histories, and the capacity to put down 3% may generally qualify for a conventional loan guaranteed by Fannie Mae or Freddie Mac. These two government-sponsored enterprises buy and sell the majority of conventional mortgages in the United States.

Borrowers are typically required to make a 20% down payment to avoid the need for private mortgage insurance (PMI). Some lenders also offer conventional loans with no private mortgage insurance and low down payments.

2. Conforming Mortgage Loans

Conforming loans are subject to the federal government's maximum loan limitations. These restrictions differ based on where you reside. The Federal Housing Finance Agency established the conforming loan limit (CLL) for one-unit homes at $548,250 for 2021.

However, the FHFA establishes a higher maximum loan limit in some areas (for example, New York City or San Francisco). Because home prices in these high-cost areas are at least 115 percent or higher than the baseline loan limit, this is the case.

3. Non-conforming Mortgage Loans

Due to loan amounts or underwriting guidelines, non-conforming loans are generally not sold or purchased by Fannie Mae or Freddie Mac. The most prevalent sort of non-conforming loan is a jumbo loan. Jumbo loans are so-called because their loan amounts often surpass conforming lending restrictions.

4. Government-Insured Federal Housing Administration (FHA) Loans

When low-to-moderate-income buyers cannot qualify for a conventional loan, they typically turn to FHA-insured loans (FHA). Borrowers can properly put down as little as 3.5 percent of the home's purchase price.

FHA loan credit score requirements are less stringent than conventional loan requirements. On the other hand, the FHA does not make direct loans; instead, it guarantees loans made by FHA-approved lenders. FHA loans have one disadvantage. For the life of the loan, all borrowers pay an upfront and yearly mortgage insurance premium (MIP), which is a form of mortgage insurance that protects the lender from borrower failure.

FHA loans are ideal for borrowers with low-to-moderate income who cannot qualify for a conventional loan or cannot afford a large down payment. A minimum FICO score of 500 is properly required to qualify for a 10% down payment on an FHA loan, and a minimum FICO score of 580 is required to qualify for a 3.5 percent down payment.

5. Government-Insured Veterans Affairs (V.A.) Loans

The U.S. Department of Veterans Affairs (V.A.) guarantees home buyer loans for qualified military service members, veterans, and spouses. Borrowers can finance the entire loan amount with no money down. Other benefits include lower closing costs (which may be paid by the seller), lower interest rates, and no need for PMI or MIP.

To help mitigate taxpayer expenses, V.A. loans demand a financing charge, a percentage of the loan amount. The funding fee is determined by your military service category as well as the loan amount. The funding fee is waived for the following service members:

- Veterans who receive V.A. benefits as a result of a service-related disability
- Veterans would be eligible for V.A. disability benefits for a service-related disability if they did not receive retirement or active duty pay.
- Survivors of veterans who were murdered in the line of duty or who have a service-related condition
- A service member with a planned or memorandum rating is eligible for compensation due to a pre-discharge claim.
- A Purple Heart recipient V.A. loans are ideal for eligible active military personnel or veterans, as well as their spouses, who want highly competitive terms and a mortgage product tailored to their specific financial needs.

6. Government-Insured U.S. Department of Agriculture Loans

The USDA guarantees loans to assist low-income buyers in rural areas in achieving homeownership. Qualified borrowers can obtain these loans with little to no money down if the property meets the USDA's eligibility requirements.

USDA loans are ideal for first-time homebuyers in eligible rural areas with low household income, little money saved for a down payment. They cannot qualify for a conventional loan product.

Fixed-Rate Mortgages

Mortgage terms, such as repayment period length, have a significant impact on how a lender prices your loan and determines your interest rate. Fixed-rate loans are exactly what their name suggests: they have a fixed interest rate. A loan with a fixed interest rate for the loan term typically ranges from 10 to 30 years.

If you properly want to pay off your mortgage faster and can afford a higher monthly payment, a fixed-rate loan with a shorter term (say, 15 or 20 years) can save you time and money. You'll also be able to accumulate equity in your home much more quickly.

Your monthly payments will be higher if you choose a shorter fixed-term mortgage over a longer-term loan. You can verify that your budget can handle the higher payments by crunching the figures. You may also want to think about other goals, such as saving for retirement or establishing an emergency fund.

Fixed-rate mortgages are ideal for buyers who plan to live in their homes for an extended period.

Other financial obligations may be met if you take out a 30-year fixed loan. For example, suppose you have the appetite for a little risk and the resources and discipline to pay off your mortgage faster. In that case, a 15-year fixed loan can save you significantly on interest and cut your repayment period in half.

Adjustable-Rate Mortgages

Adjustable-rate mortgages feature a fixed interest rate for the first ten years, but after that, the rate changes depending on market circumstances. If you cannot make a higher monthly mortgage payment once the interest rate resets, these loans are risky.

Some ARM products include a rate cap, which limits your monthly mortgage payment to a specific amount. If that's the case, do the math to ensure that you'll be able to handle any payment increases up to that point. Because market conditions—and your finances—can change, don't count on being able to sell or refinance your home before your ARM resets.

An ARM is an excellent option if you don't intend to stay in a house over the first fixed-rate period or know you'll refinance before the loan resets. Why? In the early years of repayment, ARM interest rates are often lower than fixed rates, so you might potentially save thousands of dollars in interest payments.

First-Time Assistance Programs

First-time homebuyers can get help from special programs sponsored by states or local housing authorities. Many of these programs are accessible to buyers based on their income or financial need. These programs, which typically offer down payment assistance in the form of grants, can also save first-time borrowers a significant amount of money on closing costs.

The United States Department of Housing and Urban Development (HUD) provides a state-by-state list of first-time homebuyer programs. First, choose your state, then "Homebuying Assistance," to find a program near you.

Mortgages for First-Time Buyers

Except for first-time homebuyer aid programs, all these financing programs are accessible to all homebuyers, regardless of their first time purchasing a house. Unfortunately, many people assume that FHA loans are exclusively accessible to first-time buyers. However, repeat borrowers who have not owned a primary property for at least three years before the purchase may be eligible. 13 The best loan for your situation is determined primarily by your financial situation: Earnings, credit history and score, employment, and financial goals are all factors to consider. Mortgage lenders can help you analyze your financial situation and find the best loan products for you. They can also help you understand the qualification requirements, which can be complex.

To put you in the best possible position to obtain a mortgage and buy a home, a helpful lender or mortgage broker may also assign you homework—specific areas of your finances to improve.

Chapter 2 | Loan Types

While the variety of financing options available to first-time homebuyers may appear overwhelming, learning the fundamentals of property financing can properly save you a significant amount of time and money.

Knowing the market in which the property is located and whether or not it offers lender incentives may result in additional financial rewards for you. You can also ensure that you get the best mortgage for your needs by carefully scrutinizing your finances.

Conventional Loans

Mortgages that are not guaranteed properly by the federal government are referred to as conventional loans. They are typically fixed-rate mortgages. They are some of the most difficult mortgages to qualify for due to stricter requirements such as a larger down payment, a higher credit score, lower income-to-debt ratios, and the possibility of private mortgage insurance. However, it is usually less expensive than a federally guaranteed loan if you qualify for a conventional mortgage.

Conventional loans are properly classified into two types: conforming loans and non-conforming loans. Conforming loans follow guidelines established by government-sponsored enterprises (GSEs) such as Fannie Mae and Freddie Mac. These lenders (and others) frequently buy and package these loans before selling them on the secondary market as securities. On the other hand, conforming loans must adhere to strict guidelines to be sold on the secondary market.

In 2021, the maximum conforming loan ceiling for a conventional mortgage is $548,250. However, this figure may be higher in high-cost locations.

A loan over this amount is referred to as a jumbo loan, and it usually has a slightly higher interest rate. However, the higher risk (, the larger amount of money involved) makes these loans less appealing to the secondary market.

The lending institution underwriting the loan, typically a portfolio lender, establishes its non-conforming loan guidelines. Due to regulations, non-conforming loans cannot be sold on the secondary market.

Federal Housing Administration (FHA) Loans

The Federal Housing Administration, a division of the U.S. Department of Housing and Urban Development (HUD), provides mortgage lending services to Americans. A conventional loan has a higher down payment requirement and is more difficult to qualify for than an FHA loan. FHA loans are great for first-time homeowners since they offer lower upfront loan fees, less rigorous credit criteria, and allow for as little as 3.5 percent down payment. FHA loans are not permitted to exceed the statutory restrictions stated above.

HOWEVER, all FHA borrowers are properly required to pay a mortgage insurance premium incorporated into their monthly mortgage payments. Mortgage insurance is a policy that properly protects a mortgage lender or title holder if the borrower fails to make payments, dies, or is otherwise unable to satisfy the mortgage's contractual obligations.

V.A. Loans

Veterans Affairs loans are guaranteed by the United States Department of Veterans Affairs (V.A.). The VA does not issue loans, but it does guarantee mortgages made by authorized lenders. These assurances enable veterans to get advantageous terms on house loans.

V.A. loans are typically less difficult to get than traditional loans. Because lenders usually restrict the maximum V.A. loan at the same amount as traditional mortgage loans, this is the case. However, you must first obtain eligibility from the V.A. before applying for a loan. If you are accepted, the Veterans Administration will provide you a certificate of eligibility to use when applying for a loan.

Aside from these federal loan types and programs, state and local governments and organizations sponsor assistance programs to stimulate investment in certain regions.

Requirements for Equity and Income

Lenders will use the loan-to-value ratio (LTV) and debt-service coverage ratio (DSCR) from the three major credit bureaus, as well as your FICO score, to determine the amount they're willing to loan you and the interest rate. 5 The amount of actual or implied equity available in the collateral being financed is the LTV. For home purchases, LTV is calculated by dividing the loan amount by the home purchase price. Lenders believe that the more money you put down, the less likely you will default on the loan. The larger the LTV, the greater the chance of default, and hence the higher the interest rate charged by lenders.

The DSCR evaluates your ability to repay the loan. Lenders estimate your chances of defaulting on your mortgage by dividing your monthly net income by the mortgage costs. The majority of lenders will require DSCRs greater than one. The higher the ratio, the more likely you will cover your borrowing costs and the less risk the lender will take. The higher the DSCR, the more likely the lender will negotiate the loan rate; even if the rate is lower, the lender receives a better risk-adjusted return.

As a result, you should include any type of qualifying income you can when negotiating with a mortgage lender. For example, a second part-time job or another source of income can mean the difference between qualifying for a loan and not qualifying or receiving the best possible rate.

Private Mortgage Insurance (PMI)

LTV also determines whether you need to buy private mortgage insurance (PMI). PMI protects the lender from default by transferring a portion of the loan risk to a mortgage insurer. Most lenders properly require private mortgage insurance (PMI) on loans with a loan-to-value (LTV) greater than 80%. This is any loan in which you have less than 20% equity in your home. The amount insured and the mortgage program determine the cost of mortgage insurance and how it is collected.

The majority of mortgage insurance premiums and tax and insurance escrows are collected every month. When LTV is equal to or less than 78 percent, PMI is supposed to be automatically eliminated. You may be properly able to cancel PMI after the home has appreciated enough to give you 20% equity and a specified period, such as two years.

Mortgage insurance is calculated as a lump sum by some lenders, such as the FHA, and is factored into the loan amount.

When purchasing a home, it is best not to borrow more than 80% of the property value; instead, use home equity financing or a second mortgage to put down more than 20%. The most common type of loan is an 80-10-10 mortgage. The 80 represents the first mortgage's LTV, the first ten represents the second mortgage's LTV, and the second ten represents the home's equity.

Although the second mortgage rate will be higher than the first, it should not be considerably more than the combined 90 percent LTV loan rate. With an 80-10-10 mortgage, paying for PMI may be less expensive. It also allows you to accelerate payments on the second mortgage and quickly eliminate that portion of the debt, allowing you to pay off your home faster.

Fixed-Rate Mortgages vs. Floating-Rate Mortgages

Another consideration is whether you want a fixed-rate or floating-rate mortgage (also known as variable-rate). The interest rate on a fixed-rate mortgage does not fluctuate during the term of the loan. So, the obvious benefit of obtaining a fixed-rate loan is knowing what your monthly loan costs will be for the loan duration. And, if interest rates are currently low, you've secured a favorable rate for a long time.

A floating-rate mortgage, also known as an interest-only mortgage or an adjustable-rate mortgage (ARM), is designed to assist first-time homebuyers or those who anticipate a significant increase in income over the loan term. Floating-rate loans typically have lower introductory rates during the first few years of the loan, allowing you to qualify for more money than you would have if you had tried to get a more expensive fixed-rate loan.

Another disadvantage is that the market interest rate trajectory is unknown: If they rise, the terms of your loan will rise as well.

How Adjustable-Rate Mortgages (ARMs) Work

ARMs with terms of one, five, or seven years are the most common. When an ARM resets, it adjusts to the market rate by adding some predetermined spread (percentage) to the current U.S. Treasury rate.

Although the increase is typically restricted, an ARM adjustment may cost more than the existing fixed-rate mortgage loan to compensate the lender for giving a lower rate during the promotional period.

Interest-only loans are a form of adjustable-rate mortgage (ARM). You pay just interest rather than principle during the initial period until the loan is changed to a fixed, principal-paying loan. Paying only interest on such loans can be very beneficial for first-time borrowers because it lowers the monthly cost of borrowing and allows you to qualify for a much larger loan. However, because no principal is paid during the initial period, the loan balance remains unchanged until the principal is repaid.

Chapter 3 | Mortgages for First-Time Buyers

Except for first-time homebuyer aid programs, all of these financing programs are open to all homebuyers, whether your first or fourth time is buying a house. Unfortunately, many people believe that FHA loans are only available to first-time buyers. Still, repeat borrowers can qualify if they have not owned a primary residence for at least three years before the purchase. 13 The best loan for your situation is determined primarily by your financial situation: Your earnings, credit history and score, employment, and financial goals. Mortgage lenders can help you analyze your finances and find the best loan products for you. They can also help you understand the qualification requirements, which can be complicated.

A helpful lender or mortgage broker may also assign you homework—specific areas of your finances to improve—to put you in the best possible position to obtain a mortgage and purchase a home.

Understanding Conventional Mortgages and Loans

Conventional mortgages typically have a fixed interest rate, which means the interest rate does not change during the loan term. Banks and creditors have stricter lending requirements because the federal government does not guarantee conventional mortgages or loans.

Borrowers must, however, meet certain criteria to be eligible for these programs.

Conventional vs. Conforming

Conventional loans are frequently mislabeled as conforming mortgages or loans. While some overlap exists, the two categories are distinct. A conforming loan's underlying terms and conditions fulfill Fannie Mae and Freddie Mac's funding standards. The most significant of these, the Federal Housing Finance Agency, imposes an annual amount cap (FHFA). For example, a loan cannot exceed $548,250 in most continental United States in 2021.

As a result, while all conventional loans are conforming, not all conforming loans are conforming. An $800,000 jumbo mortgage, for example, is a conventional mortgage but not a conforming mortgage since it exceeds the amount that Fannie Mae or Freddie Mac would back.

In 2020, there will be 8.3 million homeowners with FHA-insured mortgages. As a result, the conventional mortgage secondary market is massive and extremely liquid. The vast majority of conventional mortgages are packaged into pass-through mortgage-backed securities that trade in the mortgage to be announced (TBA) market, a well-established forward market. A large portion of these traditional pass-through securities is then securitized as collateralized mortgage obligations (CMOS).

How does a Conventional Mortgage or Loan Works?

Potential borrowers must complete an official mortgage application (and usually pay an application fee), then provide the lender with the required documents so that the lender can conduct a thorough investigation into their credit history, background, and current credit score.

Required Documentation

A lender examines your assets and obligations to determine if you can make your monthly mortgage payments, which should not exceed 28 percent of your gross income. 6 The lender will also want to know if you can afford a down payment (and if so, how much), as well as additional upfront charges such as loan origination or underwriting fees, broker fees, and settlement or closing costs, which may all considerably raise the cost of a mortgage. Furthermore, the following elements must be present:

1. Proof of Income

These documents will include, but will not be limited to:

- Thirty days' worth of pay stubs displaying earnings as well as year-to-date earnings
- Federal tax properly returns for the previous two years

- Statement of all asset accounts, including checking, savings, and any investment accounts, every sixty days or quarterly.
- Forms W-2 for the previous two years

Borrowers must also show proof of any other income, such as alimony or bonuses.

2. Assets

You must produce bank and investment account statements, as well as cash reserves to demonstrate that you have adequate money for the down payment and closing fees. In addition, if you receive funds from a friend or relative to help with the down payment, you'll need gift letters to prove that it isn't a loan with no required or obligatory repayment. Almost always, these letters will need to be notarized.

3. Employment Verification

Lenders today want to make certain that they are only lending to borrowers with a consistent work history. If you have changed jobs, a lender may want to contact your previous employer. Self-employed borrowers will be required to provide extensive documentation about their business and income.

4. Other Documentation

To pull your credit report, your lender will need a copy of your driver's license or state I.D. card, as well as your Social Security number and signature.

Interest Rates for Conventional Mortgages

Interest rates on conventional loans are typically higher than those on government-backed mortgages such as FHA loans.

The interest rate on a conventional mortgage is determined by several factors, including the loan's terms—the loan's length, size, and whether the interest rate is fixed or adjustable—as well as current economic or financial market conditions. In addition, mortgage lenders set interest rates based on their expectations for future inflation; supply and demand for mortgage-backed securities also impact rates.

When the Federal Reserve makes borrowing more expensive for banks by targeting a higher federal funds rate, the higher costs are passed on to customers, and consumer loan rates, including mortgage rates, tend to rise.

Special Factors to Consider When Obtaining a Conventional Mortgage or Loan

These loans are not appropriate for everyone. Here's a breakdown of who might be eligible for a conventional mortgage and who might not.

Who May Qualify

Conventional mortgages are typically available to people with established credit, excellent credit reports, and good financial standing. Therefore, the ideal applicant should, in particular, possess the following characteristics:

Credit Score

Credit scores consider a borrower's credit history as well as the number of missed payments. A credit score of at least 680, ideally much above 700, may be necessary for acceptance. Furthermore, the higher the credit score, the lower the interest rate on loan, with those with a score of 740 or higher receiving the best terms.

Debt-to-Income

A debt-to-income ratio is acceptable. This is properly calculated by dividing your monthly debt payments by your monthly income. The debt-to-income ratio should ideally be about 36% and should not be higher than 43%. To put it another way, you should not spend more than 36% of your monthly income on debt payments.

Down Payment

A purchase price of at least 25% of the buying price of the home is easily accessible. Of course, lenders can and do accept less, but if they do, borrowers are frequently required to obtain private mortgage insurance and pay monthly premiums until they have at least 20% equity in their home.

Furthermore, conventional mortgages are frequently the best or only option for homebuyers looking for an investment property, a second home, or a property worth more than $500,000.

Who May Not Qualify

In general, those just starting in life, those with a little more debt than usual, and those with a low credit score frequently have difficulty qualifying for conventional loans. These mortgages would be especially difficult to obtain for those who have:

- Have you properly filed for bankruptcy or been foreclosed on within the last seven years?
- DTIs of more than 43% for credit scores less than 650
- A down payment of less than 20%, or even 10%, of the home's purchase price is acceptable.

However, if you are denied a mortgage, make sure to get the bank's reasons in writing. You may be eligible for other programs that can assist you in obtaining a mortgage.

You may be eligible for an FHA loan if you have no credit history and are a first-time homebuyer. This is because FHA loans are properly designed for first-time home buyers. As a result, FHA loans have their own set of qualifications and credit requirements, as well as a lower down payment.

Chapter 4 | Jumbo vs. Conventional Mortgages: An Overview

Borrowers purchase homes using two types of financing: jumbo mortgages and conventional mortgages. Both require homeowners to meet certain eligibility criteria, such as minimum credit scores, income thresholds, repayment ability, and down payment requirements. In addition, both mortgage products are not backed by GSEs such as Fannie Mae and Freddie Mac, the Federal Housing Administration (FHA), the United States Department of Veterans Affairs (V.A.), or the USDA Rural Housing Service. As a result, they are fundamentally different, even though they are both used to secure property.

Jumbo mortgages are used to buy properties with high purchase prices, frequently in the millions of dollars. On the other hand, conventional mortgages are designed to meet the needs of the average homebuyer and can be either conforming or non-conforming. Continue reading to properly find out more about these two kinds of mortgage products.

Jumbo Mortgages

As previously stated, jumbo mortgages are loans used to finance the purchase of the real estate. Unlike traditional mortgages, these loans are intended for high-priced properties. As a result, jumbo mortgages are frequently used to finance luxury homes and those in hotly competitive local real estate markets.

These non-conforming mortgages are referred to as jumbo loans. As a result, they are not subject to Federal Housing Finance Agency (FHFA) loan restrictions and are not guaranteed properly by Fannie Mae or Freddie Mac. Regardless, many lenders adhere to the Consumer Financial Protection Bureau's guidelines for qualified mortgages (CFPB). They exceed the maximum conforming loan limit in their respective counties. Well-off borrowers with special needs or interest-only mortgages that culminate in balloon payments at the end of the loan term, where the entire borrowed balance is due at the end of the loan term, are two other factors that may disqualify them from being conforming loans.

To qualify for a jumbo loan, borrowers must have an excellent credit score. Borrowers should also earn more money. After all, keeping up with regular mortgage payments and other associated costs is expensive. Furthermore, borrowers must have low debt-to-income (DTI) ratios because lending requirements have become more stringent in the aftermath of the financial crisis.

Jumbo loan interest rates have historically been much higher than traditional mortgage rates. Even though the gap has narrowed, they remain slightly higher. Down payments were also structured similarly, reaching as high as 30% at one point. However, jumbo loans with down payments ranging from 10% to 15% are becoming more common. Higher interest rates and down payments were traditionally used to offset the higher degree of risk associated with these mortgage products, which the GSEs above do not guarantee.

Conventional Mortgages

Conventional mortgages are provided by private lenders such as banks and other financial institutions such as credit unions and mortgage companies. Borrowers must make a down payment, have a minimum credit score, a certain income level, and a low DTI ratio, like with jumbo loans, and GSEs do not guarantee these loans.

Unlike jumbo loans, conventional mortgages can be conforming or non-conforming. The FHFA establishes conforming loan limits. Fannie Mae and Freddie Mac also set the underwriting guidelines for these loans. In 2021, the national maximum for conforming conventional loans for a single-family home is $548,250, up from $510,400 in 2020.

However, not all mortgages follow these guidelines, and those that do are referred to as conventional non-conforming loans. Because the government does not back them, lenders determine eligibility and terms, making them more difficult to qualify for than conforming mortgages. On the other hand, one benefit is that they are often less expensive.

Special Considerations

Fannie Mae and Freddie Mac will package, purchase, and resell almost any mortgage that meets their conforming loan criteria. These guidelines consider a borrower's credit score and history, debt-to-income (DTI) ratio, loan-to-value (LTV) ratio, and one other critical factor: loan size. The government sets these maximum figures.

Because federal agencies do not guarantee jumbo loans, lenders risk more by making them available.

You'll have to meet more stringent credit requirements if you want to get a loan. As previously stated, to qualify, you must meet certain minimum requirements, which include:

Proof of Income: Bring two years' worth of tax returns or similar documentation to show that you have a consistent and reliable source of income. Lenders will also want to see that you have enough liquid assets to cover your mortgage payments for at least six months.

Credit score and history: You must have a credit score of at least 580 (called "fair") before a lender would accept you for a conventional mortgage, but lenders are unlikely to approve you for a jumbo mortgage if your credit score falls below 670.

Debt-to-Income ratio (DTI): To qualify for a conventional mortgage, you must have a debt-to-income ratio of 43 percent or less (your monthly debt obligations divided by your monthly income). Because jumbo mortgages are so large, lenders typically prefer a lower DTI.

Chapter 5 | What Is an Assumable Mortgage?

A form of financial arrangement in which the existing owner transfers the terms of an ongoing mortgage to a buyer is known as an assumable mortgage. By taking on the previous owner's remaining debt, the buyer can avoid getting their mortgage.

Understanding Assumable Mortgages

Many homebuyers obtain a mortgage from a lending institution to finance the purchase of a home or property. The contractual agreement for loan repayment specifies the borrower's obligation to pay both interest and principal to the lender.

Later, the mortgage may be transferred to the new homeowner if the homeowner decides to sell their home. In this case, the original mortgage can be assumed.

A homebuyer can assume the current principal balance, interest rate, repayment period, and any other contractual terms of the seller's mortgage with an assumable mortgage. Thus, rather than going through the arduous process of obtaining a loan from a bank, a buyer can take over an existing mortgage. In addition, there may be a cost-saving advantage if current interest rates are higher than the interest rate on the assumable loan.

Borrowing becomes more expensive during an interest rate rise. If this occurs, borrowers will face high-interest rates on any loans that are approved. As a result, an assumable mortgage is more likely to have a lower interest rate, which buyers find appealing. Rising interest rates will not affect the assumable mortgage if it has a fixed interest rate.

Types of Assumable Mortgages

The Federal Housing Administration, the Veteran's Administration (V.A.), and the United States Department of Agriculture offers assumable mortgages (USDA). Conventional loans, on the other hand, are unassumable. In addition, buyers who want to assume a seller's mortgage must meet certain requirements and obtain approval from the mortgage's sponsoring agency.

FHA Loans

FHA loans are assumable if both transacting parties meet the requirements for the assumption. The seller, for example, must use the property as their primary residence. Before applying for an individual FHA loan, buyers must first confirm that the FHA loan is assumable. Next, the seller's lender will confirm that the buyer meets all criteria, including creditworthiness. If the loan is approved, the buyer will take over the mortgage. However, the seller is still liable for the loan until and unless they are released from it.

V.A. Loans

The Department of Veterans Affairs properly offers mortgages to qualified military members and military spouses. The buyer does not have to be a member of the military to qualify for a V.A. loan. However, the lender and the regional V.A. loan office must approve the buyer for the loan assumption, and most buyers who assume V.A. loans are military members.

For loans originated before March 1, 1988, buyers may freely assume the V.A. loan.

Put another way, and the buyer does not need the V.A.'s or the lender's approval to assume the mortgage.

USDA Loans

They usually feature cheap loan rates and no down payment. To qualify for a USDA loan, the buyer must fulfill the normal standards, including credit and income requirements, and get USDA title approval. The buyer can accept the current interest rate and loan terms or negotiate new rates and terms. However, even if the buyer meets all of the criteria and is approved, the mortgage cannot be assumed if the seller has delinquent payments.

Advantages and Disadvantages of Assumable Mortgages

In a high-interest rate environment, the benefits of acquiring an assumable mortgage are limited to the loan's existing mortgage balance or home equity. Alternatively, the buyer will need to secure the additional funds with a separate mortgage.

When the purchase price of the house exceeds the mortgage debt by a substantial amount, the buyer must seek a new loan. The interest rate might be substantially higher than the estimated loan, depending on the buyer's credit history and current interest rates.

If the buyer has a lot of equity in their property, a buyer would usually take out a reverse mortgage on top of the first one. The buyer may be required to obtain a second loan from a lender other than the seller's lender, which could cause complications if both lenders do not cooperate. Having two loans also increases the risk of default, especially if one has a higher interest rate.

However, if the seller's home equity is low, the buyer may find the assumable mortgage appealing. For example, if the home is worth $250,000 and the assumable mortgage balance is $210,000, the buyer only needs to put down $40,000 to purchase it. If the purchaser has this amount in cash, they may pay the seller without securing another credit line.

Special Considerations for Assumable Mortgages

The buyer and seller do not influence whether an assumable mortgage may be transferred or not. The original mortgage lender must authorize the mortgage assumption before either side may sign off on the agreement. The homeowner must apply for the assumable loan and fulfill the lender's conditions, such as sufficient assets and creditworthiness.

If the application is accepted, the buyer takes possession of the property and begins making the required monthly payments to the bank. However, if the lender denies the transfer, the seller will have to locate another buyer prepared to accept his mortgage and has good credit.

A third party's acceptance of a mortgage does not free the seller of the obligation to repay the debt. As a result, the seller may be held liable for any defaults, which may impact their credit rating. To avoid this, the seller must waive their responsibility in writing at the time of assumption, and the lender must confirm the request, thus freeing the seller of any loan responsibilities.

Conclusion

To obtain a mortgage, the borrower must submit an application to a lender and information about their financial history, demonstrating that they can repay the loan. Borrowers can use the services of a mortgage broker to help them choose a lender.

The procedure is divided into several steps. Borrowers may first seek pre-qualification. Pre-qualifying entails providing a bank or lender with an overview of your overall financial picture, including your debt, income, and assets. The lender will go over everything with you and estimate how much you can properly expect to borrow.

The next step is to get preapproval. To get preapproved, you must fill out an official mortgage application and supply the lender with all relevant paperwork so that the lender may perform a comprehensive investigation into your financial history and current credit rating. Furthermore, you will be granted a written conditional commitment for a certain loan amount, which will allow you to seek a property in that price range or below.

After you've discovered a house you want, the next step is to obtain a loan commitment, which a bank will only provide after it has authorized both you as the borrower and the property in question. That is, the property has been appraised at or above the sales price.

When the borrower and lender agree on the terms of the home loan, the lender places a lien as collateral for the loan. The lender has the power to smoothly repossess the property if the borrower fails to make payments.

Visit And Buy the Other Books of This Author

Happy Saint Patrick's Day: Saint Patrick's Day Planner/Journal with 8.5x11 inches and 100 Pages

https://www.amazon.com/dp/B09BY841SZ

St. Patrick's Day: Saint Patrick's Day Planner/Journal with 8.5x11 inches and 100 Pages

https://www.amazon.com/dp/B09BY7XWGD

Happy Easter: Easter Egg Patterns Worksheet: 8.5x11 Inches 60 Pages

https://www.amazon.com/dp/B09BT2B6F3

Easter Hunt Activity Happy Easter: Easter Hunt Activity Journal | Notebook size 8.5x11 60 Pages

https://www.amazon.com/dp/B09BY7XWKL

Easter Day Spring Writing Assignment worksheet: Easter Day Spring Writing Assignment worksheet | 8.5x11 60 Pages | Spring Worksheet

https://www.amazon.com/dp/B09BY5HNVB

Cinco De Mayo: Large Updated Organizer with Daily Spreads For 2 Months with Cover Paperback https://www.amazon.com/dp/B09BY8178L

Taking full charge of your finance: Easy Guide to Personal Finance

https://www.amazon.com/Taking-full-charge-your-finance/dp/B099C8S85Z

Sure, Steps to Wealth Creation: How to Build Wealth from Nothing

https://www.amazon.com/Sure-Steps-Wealth-Creation-Nothing/dp/B099C3GNQH

All You Need to Know About Cryptocurrency: Understanding Risk and Reward in Investing

https://www.amazon.com/Need-Know-About-Cryptocurrency-Understanding/dp/B099C3GNML

Eliminating Your Debt in 12 (x) Easy Steps and Keep Them Off: A Practical Guide to Eliminating Your Debt Forever!

https://www.amazon.com/Eliminating-Your-Debt-Easy-Steps/dp/B099BZX4FX

NLP For Beginners

https://www.amazon.com/NLP-Beginners-RS-Johnson-ebook/dp/B098JBH28Q

Credit Repair Secrets

https://www.amazon.com/Credit-Repair-Secrets-RS-Johnson/dp/B098JH79X2

<-END->

www.ingramcontent.com/pod-product-compliance
Lightning Source LLC
Chambersburg PA
CBHW030038230526
45472CB00002B/573